Crystal Healing

How Crystal healing works, crystal therapy, the human energy field, gemstones, and how to use crystals for healing and increased energy!

Table of Contents

Introduction 1
Chapter 1: Crystals and Crystal Therapy 2
Chapter 2: How crystal therapy works 5
Chapter 3: Crystals and their healing properties 9
Chapter 4: Healing crystals with high energy 14
Chapter 5: Healing crystals for spiritual and mental Health 17
Chapter 6: Healing crystals for Holistic and Physical health 20
Chapter 7: A Complete List of the Different Healing Crystals and their Uses 25
Chapter 8: Crystals vs. Gemstones 37
Chapter 9: How to Cleanse Crystals? 40
Chapter 10: How to Clear your Chakras to Make Crystal Healing More Effective 43
Chapter 11: Different Ways that Crystals can be Used for Healing 46
Chapter 12: Toxic Crystals to Avoid 49
Chapter 13: Crystals and their Use in Religions 51
Chapter 14: Crystals for Psychic Healing 53
Conclusion 56

Introduction

I want to thank you and congratulate you for picking up the book, *"Crystal Healing"*.

This is the recently updated 2nd edition. This book has been edited, updated, and improved through adding a range of new information on the topic of crystal healing! It can now be considered an absolutely complete guide to healing with crystals!

This book contains helpful information about crystal healing, what it is, and how to use it for improved health and wellbeing.

You will soon learn about the different uses of crystal healing, and the theories behind how it works. While crystal healing is not a 'complete' method for curing diseases and ailments, it can be used alongside traditional treatments for improved benefits. Further to this, it can be used to improve simple ailments and issues such as headaches, insomnia, and a lack of energy.

You will discover the different crystals and gemstones that are available, along with the benefits of each. There are a huge range of crystals to choose from, each with their own positive effects on the body.

This book will also explain to you tips and techniques that will allow you to properly take care of your crystals. You will learn which chakras respond to certain crystals, and how to use the crystals properly in conjunction with these chakras.

Upon completion of this book, you will be well prepared to begin implementing crystal healing in your own life!

Thanks again for taking the time to read this book, I hope you enjoy it!

Chapter 1:
Crystals and Crystal Therapy

What are Crystals?

Crystals are elements that are formed through solidified chemicals which contain internal molecular and atomic arrangements with repeated patterns and are bordered by plane sides externally. Because of their internal density, crystals form different geometrical shapes. Crystals are naturally beautiful to look at and so they are an important and primary aesthetic component in jewelry and accessories. They also exhibit reflective properties which enable them to be utilized in the optical and electronic industries.

At present, crystals play a major role in almost any aspect of modern technology. More importantly, people believe in their healing properties and mystic powers which make them popular in alternative medicine. Believers and practitioners claim that crystals contain energy which can be channeled to a person or thing and crystals also possess the power to neutralize and remove negative energy and convert it to positive. Although not yet proven scientifically, people have since incorporated crystals into their healthy lifestyle, especially during meditation and medical recovery.

Healing crystals give off vibrations which are compatible with human chakras. These vibrations can help equalize the positive and negative energies in the person – their yin and yang. When these crystals are placed appropriately, they reverberate with healing frequencies which can affect emotional, physical, spiritual and mental stability and condition of the person. Crystals can also inspire creativity and self-expression. They can also help with meditation and strengthen the body's immune system.

What is Crystal Therapy?

Crystal therapy or crystal healing is a form of pseudoscience that deals with the utilization of crystals and other gemstones for healing. This is also another form of alternative medicine which uses a method of placing crystals or stones on a particular body part which corresponds appropriately with the intended chakra. Other methods employ placing the crystals around the body to create an "energy field" which then enables the person to become surrounded with healing energies.

Traditional and alternative medicine both tap into the concept that energies surround every element in the physical and supernatural worlds, and that crystals are the perfect mediums that we can utilize to balance out negative and positive energies. This is basically the reason why crystals are often used in popular health clinics and health spas.

As an alternative medicine, crystal therapy lacks scientific evidence to claim the effectiveness of such methods. However, a lot of people still believe that crystals and gemstones possess healing and spiritual properties which can be activated in various ways. There are different ways to utilize a crystal. It can be worn as an accessory or carried inside a pouch. It can be placed anywhere as long as the vibrations are felt for healing purposes. Practitioners and healers also place the stones on a specific body part corresponding to the client's aura and chakra for maximized healing and relaxing effects.

It is important to note that in crystal therapy, everything about the crystal is very important. The textures, shapes, and colors of crystals are very meaningful. People create crystal elixirs by soaking a particular crystal in a glass full of water for a few hours. Crystals used for healing are employed during meditation and divination rituals for maximum healing powers. In choosing a crystal, one can feel which specific crystal a person is attracted to. An open mind and heart can bring forth the power of a crystal towards the person. However, it is not the chemical component of a crystal which makes it beneficial. It is the belief that the crystal is a medium or a tool that connects both the physical and supernatural worlds.

Chapter 2:
How crystal therapy works

Crystal therapy is a primordial kind of art characterized by placing crystals and gemstones over chakra points on the body. These points are thought to correspond to a specific color. When a crystal or a gemstone of similar color is placed on top of that chakra point, the chakra will open up, energy is aligned and the auric energy will be balanced. Practitioners of this method believe that diseases, pain and any form of discomfort and disturbance are a sign that there is something wrong with the chakra system. Once all these chakra systems are neutralized, the internal processes of the body will naturally correct itself and healing is attained.

Through resonance and vibration, light and color is channeled from the auric field to the physical body through the layers of the body and the chakra systems. Color in crystal therapy indicates which energy characteristic represents a certain frequency. When light is refracted or bent, color is produced. Where there is light there is color and these two are inseparable. One of the functions of light is color production. Such frequency of the light wave seen by the naked human eye produces a spectrum of light in a specific order similar to that of the rainbow. Red, orange, yellow, green, blue, indigo and violet are the specific colors which correspond to a chakra. Each color of crystals and gemstones should therefore be similar to each color designated to each of the seven chakras.

What are chakras?

Chakras are the seven parts of the body known as the main centers for energy flow. When one of these chakras is blocked or imbalanced, the person experiences pain, discomfort and illness. Healers will utilize crystals and quartz to improve the energy flow and neutralize imbalances. Once imbalances and blockages are corrected and aligned, the person recovers and returns to a normal state of being.

1. First Chakra: This is located at the pelvic area at the bottom part of the spine. This chakra is associated with a red color and is typically known as the gateway to the nervous system. When there's a problem with this area, the healer will place quartz crystals to release tension and physical stress from the nervous system.

2. Second Chakra: This is found near the spleen and is associated with the color Orange. When a person experiences difficulty or problems with sexual or reproductive organs, the second chakra will have to be corrected or healed.

3. Third Chakra: Solar Plexus is the third chakra and it can be found just below the navel. The color associated with this chakra is Yellow and this is where energy and physical power is stored.

4. Fourth Chakra: This chakra is found at the center of the chest and corresponds to the center or the heart. The colors associated with the fourth chakra are green and pink. When a person is suffering from relationship problems and emotional stress and imbalances caused by traumas, the fourth chakra needs to be activated and aligned. The use of rose quartz is recommended because rose quartz helps release emotional tension and relieves emotional stress.

5. Fifth Chakra: Turquoise and blue are the designated colors for the fifth chakra. This is located at the center

of the throat. Usually when the throat or the fifth chakra is blocked, the person experiences muscle tensions in the neck and shoulders as well as headaches. To relieve this problem, the throat chakra needs to be healed.

6. Sixth Chakra: The third eye is the sixth chakra and it is found in between the eyebrows. The color associated with the sixth chakra is purple. Amethyst is a perfect example of a purple gemstone which is commonly used to treat people who would want to develop their own spiritual nourishment and strengthen their intuition.

7. Seventh Chakra: The last or the seventh chakra is the top of the head or the crown center. White is the associated color. This is where the highest knowledge, highest form of healing and understanding takes place. This chakra needs to be constantly open during any crystal healing.

What Happens during Crystal therapy?

When you go to a therapist or a healer the first thing that needs to be done is consultation. The therapist will ask you about your lifestyle and medical history. You will be asked to lie down or sit on a chair and the therapist will assess if your auric condition is good or bad. Aura refers to the spiritual, emotional and mental condition of the person. If everything is balanced, the aura is clear which means the person is healthy. If it's otherwise, there should be blockages or imbalances characterized by ailments or pain. This assessment will help your therapist or your healer to diagnose the condition of your chakras and they will then choose which crystals are going to be used on you to correct any imbalances. At the start of the session, it is normal for you to feel some tingling sensations.

Some patients have even reported that issues are initially intensified before finally being released. This is normal and the therapist will be able to give you some advice on the things you are to expect and observe after the sessions.

Crystals have the ability to direct, absorb, diffuse and focus energy to neutralize imbalanced energy flow in every chakra and remove blockages to help the body return to its natural rhythm of energy flow once again. When the appropriate crystal is placed correctly over one of the chakras, the energy is linked and channeled to our glands, organs, tissues, emotions and thoughts thereby affecting our physical, emotional, spiritual and mental condition and well-being.

Chapter 3:
Crystals and their healing properties

Crystals contain healing properties. Most people often choose their birthstones over other crystals and gemstones because birthstones correspond to their zodiac signs. However, it is also beneficial to know that there are specific stones and crystals which can be very helpful in relieving a certain ailment. Here are some important details about healing crystals and gemstones that can be used to heal common ailments.

Headaches:

There are different reasons or causes of headaches. For every cause, there is a crystal which can be used for relief. Turquoise, amber and amethyst are great for headache relief when it is caused by tension. These stones need to be placed on or around the head for maximum healing. For chronic migraines, lapis lazuli is the answer which has been used for many centuries. For regular headaches, placing the Amethyst on or around the head/forehead can help relieve the symptoms.

If the situation is different like for example the headache is coupled with an upset stomach or if the headache is caused by stress, this indicates that the solar plexus chakra is imbalanced as well as the head chakra which may be a result of unsuitable food intake or stress. Moonstone and citrine is definitely helpful in balancing the solar plexus chakra.

Sleeping Problems/Insomnia:

Not all stones or crystals work for everyone. Each crystal or stone can treat sleeplessness depending on the cause. Citrine, rose quartz, amethyst and chrysoprase are used to treat sleeplessness caused by worry and tension. These stones need to be placed under the pillow or beside the bed for a relaxing and soothing effect. If difficulty sleeping is caused by an upset stomach because of overeating, moonstone and iron pyrite is recommended to calm the stomach. Lastly, if nightmares are the reason of your sleeplessness, you need a protective stone like smoky quartz and tourmaline. These stones are placed at the foot of the bed to promote restful and peaceful sleep. To chase or remove any feelings and thoughts of being unwelcomed, labradorite is recommended.

Sexual Problems:

Sexual problems such as the lack of libido or sexual drive can be associated with the emotional stability of the person. Such emotional conditions and imbalances can affect the libido or sexual drive of a person. The blocked sexual energy can be opened and released with the help of red garnet and fluorite which are greatly helpful in restoring and stimulating passion once again.

Low Energy:

Weariness or fatigue can be healed using yellow, orange and red crystals which promote energy increase. Examples of crystals with bright and strong colors are golden-yellow topaz, deep red garnet and golden amber. These three are the most dynamic and most stimulating crystals. Jasper, dark citrine and tiger's eye on the other hand promote practical motivation increase. To achieve an energy boost quickly throughout the whole chakra system, clear quartz crystals should be held in each hand pointing upwards while placing citrine on the solar plexus area.

Mind-Healing:

Many crystals contain healing abilities to calm and relax the mind. They promote tranquility and peace through the dissolution of emotional blockages. The stones or crystals can be placed on the body through a healing lay-out or can be worn by the person. Many green crystals are also employed to assist in the reduction of nervous and mental stress. Since green is a healing color, emerald and green jades are the two most popular healing stones used to gain mental focus and calm the nervous system. If the emotions are not stable, it needs to be detoxified and cleansed. Blue lace agate and rose quartz are recommended for this process. Amethyst helps in the production of hormones, controlling emotions and balancing mood swings. Opal is necessary for emotional stability and balance. To help you refocus your goals, reduce mental tension and burdens, and relieve stress, amethyst is the stone to be used. Amber on the other hand, is best for balancing out any endocrine and emotional imbalance as well as neutralizing the negative state of mind.

Concentration and Study Problems:

Carnelian is believed to have the ability to clear irrelevant thoughts and quartz aids concentration by giving mental clarity. To amplify thoughts, nothing is better than a lapis lazuli stone. For memory stimulation, amber and citrine are recommended. Amethyst is a very useful and powerful gemstone that aids in neural transmission. It helps the person refocus goals, achieve mental clarity and can sooth the nervous system.

When studying, fluorite is the best agent that helps in stabilizing and balancing both brain hemispheres. Sodalite, a deep blue stone on the other hand, is also a good help in communication to better understand and comprehend ideas and concepts.

Crystals for Cancer Healing:

Before anything else, the information provided here is not a substitute for prescriptions or medical care. It is still best to consult with your doctor. Crystal healing is a mere complementary method employed which is spiritual in nature. Crystals used that correspond to the chakras in the body are used to facilitate healing on the body part with tumor or cancer. For breast cancers, pink crystals are used and are placed on the heart center chakra. Avoid red stones and green stones as red stones promote aggressive behavior and green stones indicate growth that may somehow promote tumor growth.

Energizing Stones:

Citrine and Yellow-Topaz are good examples of seasonal stones which are good at energizing people. They possess sun energies which are beneficial in alleviating negative thoughts and depression. When a person is suffering from SAD or Seasonal Affective Disorder, wearing these energizers on dark days will greatly help uplift the moods of the person wearing it. Corals and pearls on the other hand, are cooler stones which are best worn or carried during the summer season. Turquoise and emeralds are best during spring time and opals and sapphires are best during autumn. Yellow Topaz and Citrine are hot stones and so they are best worn during winter.

Memory Enhancers:

There are specific stones which are used as memory enhancers. They are believed to have the ability to absorb and retain information better than other stones. Red stones such as garnets, carnelians and rubies are good at holding on to information. It is best used when reviewing for an exam or memorizing details. During classes, if you have these stones with you, the stones will absorb and store information and they will also help you stay focused and engrossed during lectures. It is best to have the memory-enhancing stones with you during your examination day.

Chapter 4:
Healing crystals with high energy

Crystals and gemstones are believed to have specific properties that may or may not be beneficial to the person who wears it. Every gemstone corresponds to an astrological sign and because of this many people often choose their birth stones over other gemstones. At this point, it is important to note however, that birthstones can be mixed with other important stones. There are numerous stones used to attract a love partner, while others are used to dispel fear, illnesses, and to balance out energy fields within the auric field of the person.

Here are some of the most important crystals and gemstones used to amplify positive energies, convert negative to positive energies and to elude negative energies:

Agate: The primary use of Agate is to balance the negative and positive tendencies and energies of a person. It is another type of chalcedony. It has a variety of colors and each color is used to strengthen the mind and the body. It converts negative energy to positive, and removes and cleanses toxins from the body. Agate also has the ability to fortify the earth's connection to the body. In times of difficulty in acceptance, Agate has the properties which enable the person to accept circumstances, discern the truth and be courageous.

Amber: Amber is not a crystal in the strict sense of the word. It is actually a resin from fossilized pine trees during the prehistoric period. It is one of the best healing stones because it has the ability to suck up negative energies which will then enable the body to heal itself. When combined with golden light that is solidified, amber becomes alive electrically. To release the negative energies, amber needs to be placed on certain areas of the body which are imbalanced and painful. This helps remove the feeling of discomfort and pain. Once the negative energies are absorbed, amber turns dull or clouded. It has the ability to soothe, harmonize and heal. With the help of amber, Kundalini awakening is stabilized and the altruistic nature is activated.

Diamond: It is one of the Stones with highest frequency of energy. Diamond dispels negative energy and makes the spirit and the body both purified. It is the reflection of the person's desires in the highest consciousness. It improves the brain functions and aligns the cranial bones. It is a master healer which removes negativity, amplifying the complete spectrum of energies in the mind, body and spirit. Diamond attracts purity, innocence, abundance, faithfulness and higher self.

Gem Silica: This mineral with a clear high-blue color gives off active compassion to the person who wears it. It possesses the female (yin) energies which is great for emotional imbalances. It reduces female problems and enhances female vitality. It is an excellent healer of heart problems caused by loss, hurt, fear and guilt. When it reacts with copper, it removes pain and heat (arthritis, inflammation and fever).

Gold: It attracts positive vibes or energy while energizing and purifying the body. It enhances circulation and fortifies the nervous system. It also aids in regenerating the tissues, balances brain hemispheres, and improves the chakra of the heart. Gold converts positive energy into aura which is good for enhancing male aspects, personal realization, and solar energy.

Quartz Crystal: This is one of the most powerful crystals known to dispel the powers of negativity. It activates all spectrums of energy on all levels of consciousness. It dispels negative energy into your very own field as well as in your environment. It has the ability to activate, receive, transmit, store and amplify energy. This is one of the best tools in meditation. It greatly improves communication with the higher self. Quartz is excellent for healers and is an excellent tool for therapy.

Topaz: This is most popularly called the Stone of the Century. The power of Topaz is to detoxify the body; to awaken, inspire and warm abundance by passing on potent assistance to regenerate tissues, and to strengthen every gland and organ in the body. Golden Topaz is the most powerful solar/yellow plexus gem with electromagnetic properties. A high level, steady and strong gem of this kind promotes mental clarity, perceptivity, focus, confidence, high-level concepts, stamina and personal power. It aids in fears, worries, insomnia, mood swings, depression, nervous system problems, stomach anxiety and exhaustion. This gem is best recommended for teachers, water signs, stressful work environments, things that manifest higher self-realization.

Chapter 5:
Healing crystals for spiritual and mental Health

Some crystals possess the ability to heal the mental and spiritual imbalances of man. There are those used to strengthen the spiritual connection between the ethereal bodies and the physical body. Other stones are believed to enable man to explore deeper and higher realms of both the physical and subconscious worlds. So, here are some of the most popular stones for mental and spiritual health.

Agate: There is a specific type of Agate that can enhance mental health. The Fire Agate is a kind of fire stone (called such because of the fire-like glow inside the stone) which is used to improve creativeness, fortify the intellect, and bring about fortitude and courage.

Amber: Helps relieve the person of being absent-minded while making the intellect spiritualized.

Amethyst: It aids mental disorders. At all levels of consciousness, amethyst regenerates and purifies. It also brings human nature to a higher form of consciousness making it a very powerful tool in spiritual enhancement. It is important in meditations because it improves psychic capabilities and it breaks into illusions. Amethyst contains strong protective properties and channeling powers. It is an excellent tool for bringing forth divine love, intuition, inspiration and healing.

Bloodstone: It has a stimulating effect on the kundalini movement and a source of inspiration, intuition, idealism, altruism, spiritual solidarity and inner guidance.

Carnelian: As a good balancing stone, Carnelian aids in revitalizing the mental, emotional and physical aspects of a person. It aligns the ethereal and physical aspects of the body. It also improves the person's familiarity with the inner self and aids in concentration.

Chrysocolla: Subconscious imbalances are cleared with chrysocollas. It reduces guilt, phobias, fears and tensions.

Emerald: Deeper spiritual insight can be gained through this stone. Dreams are also improved and it attracts balance, healing, love, tranquility, kindness, and patience. Emerald is also an excellent balancer of emotions.

Heliodor: It contains revitalizing properties which aid in finding out purpose in life. It helps in overcoming resentment and fear by protecting the person from depression and over-analysis of a situation.

Iolite: This is the leadership stone. It is very colorful but most iolites are bluish to lavender in color. It is focused on control. It does not allow others to trample you or your emotions to overcome you. It aids in asserting leadership roles and you will greatly be accepted as a leader if you wear this. It is good for finding life's purpose by understanding the reasons why we are here and who we really are. It attracts self-confidence, truth and inner strength. Blue iolite: friendships; Purple iolite: sexual and family relationships; grey iolite: professional relationships.

Labradorite: This stone is best in enhancing lucid dreams. It enhances the mind and magnifies vision. When placed under the pillow, the person will enjoy a restful sleep and improved dream recall. It improves psychic powers and wisdom.

Obsidian: Possesses male subtle energies that can attract adventurers of the spirituality. Spiritual energy is often grounded into a physical plane. Negativity is dispersed by this stone. It also aids in clearing subconscious blockages and reduce stress. It attracts a deeper kind of awareness and understanding into the realms of silence and voids encouraging detachment but coupled with warmth, love and wisdom. Obsidians are naturally formed volcanic glass and different kinds attract different values and contain different meanings and uses.

Pearl: The white variety is especially important. It is an organic gem and it is best worn without any other gemstones or crystals. It symbolizes innocence, faith, purity of mind and heart. Since pearls are found in the sea, they contain fluid and lunar elements which are best suited for water signs. It is good for the absorption of emotions, thoughts, and the solar plexus chakra can certainly benefit from this gem. Pearl frequently cleanses and it helps rebound low anger and integrity to the user.

Silver: It is best for mental processes. It brings forth a desire to change by being aware of the problems and traumas and by fortifying faith in the higher self. It is also an excellent conductor of energy. Since it is somehow related to the moon, it improves the female subconscious aspect, speech and balances emotions.

Sunstone: It is a kind of Aventurine feldspar with a metallic sheen colored gold-orange. It helps rejuvenate and uplift the spirit. It attracts life force, protection and grounding.

Chapter 6:
Healing crystals for Holistic and Physical health

A lot of Stones, crystals and gems exhibit multiple uses and important properties. A lot more are being discovered every time a stone is utilized. There are indeed physical healing properties of stones known to benefit mankind but it is important to note that whatever information is supplied in this book is not actually healthcare advice or prescriptions. These are guides in finding your inner self worth and healing. Medical attention and therapy are greatly encouraged for those who experience serious medical issues. Crystals however can be used alongside traditional treatment for enhanced benefits.

Agate: Agate is an example of an excellent healing stone. It is energetic and grounded. It helps the colon to function properly. It also facilitates proper functioning of the lymphatic and circulatory systems and maintains normal pulse rate and pancreatic processes.

Alexandrite: This color-changing crystal is very rare and beautiful. It is an excellent facilitator of external and internal regenerating processes of the body. It also influences the immune systems positively, as well as the pancreas and the spleen. It promotes holistic health by rebuilding the body, mind and spirit.

Amazonite: It is good for the nervous system. It has a soothing effect and it can strengthen the physical body, most especially the heart. It also helps to align the ethereal aspect of the body to the mind.

Amber: Affects the heart, spleen and the endocrine system positively.

Amethyst: It fortifies both the immune and the endocrine systems while affecting the activity of the right brain positively, along with the pituitary gland and the pineal gland. It also energizes the blood and cleanses it.

Aquamarine: It helps to strengthen the kidneys, reduce fluid retention in the body, and improves the performance of the thyroid, spleen and liver.

Bloodstone: A form of Chalcedony. It oxygenates and fortifies the blood stream; improves mental and physical vivacity; balances iron deficiencies; strengthens the bone marrow, heart and spleen; relieves mental and emotional stress; and contains strong physical healing powers.

Carnelian: A form of Chalcedony and a very powerful and highly developed mineral healer. It improves functions of the pancreas, gall bladder, kidneys, liver and lungs. It helps energize the blood and facilitates regeneration of tissues.

Chrysocolla: It is a stone recommended for women. It relieves menstrual cramps and PMTs while fortifying feminine qualities. It helps prevent digestive problems such as ulcers, and improves arthritic conditions. It strengthens the thyroid and the lungs and helps to improve metabolism.

Chrysoprase: It balances and calms nerve patterns which aid in sexual frustrations, imbalances, and problems in fertility.

Citrine: Another form of Quartz. It is an energizing and warming crystal which gives off positive vibes to the gall bladder, kidneys, liver, colon, heart and digestive organs. It helps regenerate the tissues; removes self-destructive tendencies; improves the natural healing process of the body; improves self-esteem; and aligns the body with the more powerful higher form of self. It attracts hope, abundance, cheerfulness and light-heartedness.

Dioptase: A deep green mineral with a tinge of blue is good for the heart. It improves and fortifies the cardiovascular and central nervous systems. It helps normalize blood pressure and relieves heart troubles. Dioptase also helps nervous stomachs and ulcers.

Emerald: This is known as the Stone of Unconditional Love. It is a very powerful deep green stone of the variety of beryl. It has immense powers to strengthen the kidneys, heart, immune system, liver and nervous system. It boosts the mind, body and spirit. Subtle bodies are aligned with the help of emeralds.

Fluorite: It is one of the most powerful healing stones. It absorbs and gathers vital nutrients that benefit the spleen and the blood vessels. It helps in creating strong bones and teeth. It calms the nerves and balances out excess energy. It is best in clearing the mind for a beautiful and revitalizing sleep.

Galena: This stone is best used in fighting infection and improving lung functions.

Garnet: It is a good purificator of the blood stream. It has strong purifying and revitalizing properties which aid in the regeneration of the body's internal and external processes. It also aligns imperfections in the body and stimulates the pituitary gland. Emotional imbalances and sex drive problems are also balanced out with the use of Garnet. It elicits compassion, enhanced imagination and love. For people with low self-confidence, garnet is the best stone for them for it brings forth courage.

Heliodor: This is believed to contain the warmth and power of the sun. It aids in intestine and stomach problems such as ulcers, eating disorders and nausea. It detoxifies the skin and the liver.

Jade: Purifies the bloods and improves the kidneys, heart and immune system. It alleviates female problems and eye disorders. It releases negative energy and attracts clarity, unconditional and divine love, modesty, wisdom, justice and courage.

Lapis Lazuli: It brings about strong skeletal systems. It reactivates the thyroid gland, revitalizes the throat, removes anxiety and tension, supplements virility, strength and vitality. It attracts good fortune, increases concentration, strong instincts, and success in love, cheerfulness, personal integrity, truth, wisdom, patience and artistic talents.

Moonstone: It is a feminine stone like the chrysocolla. It heals many parts of body such as the spleen, stomach, pituitary gland, pancreas, and lymphatic systems. It relieves female problems and aids in the process of giving birth. It reduces stress and anxiety; it balances the emotions, and improves flexibility of attitude.

Sapphire: Sapphire is an excellent healing stone for kidney and heart problems. It has a stimulating effect to the pituitary gland which helps the entire glandular system. Sapphire also promotes the alignment of the mind, body and spirit which improves psychic abilities, inspiration and understanding. It attracts love, loyalty, creativity, spirituality, willpower and fair judgment.

Tourmaline: This is coined as the New Age Stone. It balances the endocrine system; facilitates restful sleep;

revitalizes and strengthens the mind and the body; enhances and activates the mind and the body's crystalline properties; improves understanding and sensitivity; dispels negative conditions and fears; and aligns subtle bodies. This is also an excellent healer possessing electromagnetic properties that assists the person in finding courage and strength to face new challenges. It also protects the wearer against unfortunate events.

Chapter 7:
A Complete List of the Different Healing Crystals and their Uses

Agate

Also referred to as the warrior stone, this crystal aids in enhancing one's courage and confidence. The Blue Lace Agate is often used to relieve inner tension, whether it is physical or spiritual in nature. Use the Botswana Agate if you need help in overcoming nicotine addiction. It also offers an aid in releasing your repressed emotions. Meanwhile, use the Moss Agate to heal a damaged ego. The Snakeskin Agate helps you develop a more cheerful disposition.

Amazonite

This is otherwise known as the "Inspiration Stone". This crystal's soothing effect is useful particularly when you're going through a difficult emotional process. It can allay anxiety and increase your willpower. You may also use it to improve your communication skills. Furthermore, the Amazonite is effective for people suffering from neurological problems.

Ametrine

This is the result of the combination of amethyst and citrine. It is used to turn your deepest desires into reality; hence, it is perfect for visualization meditation.

Amethyst

This crystal is used by those who are seeking serenity in their thoughts. Use amethysts during meditation. You may also utilize it to ward off negative thinking and to retrain your thoughts to develop optimism. It is particularly helpful for individuals suffering from emotional blockages. The Amethyst is also recommended for people who frequently complain about migraines and arthritis. However, more than that, this crystal has the ability to enhance your intuitive powers and awaken your third eye.

Apatite

This crystal opens up your heart center. It helps you to develop compassion.

Apopholyte

Use this crystal if you want to become more attuned to your physical body, but more than that, use it to develop your attunement to life forms in the higher dimension.

Aquamarine

One of the most important uses of this crystal is in treating phobic disorders. It helps you become more stable. The Aquamarine minimizes mental tension. It also empowers you to voice out your own truth.

Aventurine

Use this crystal to purify both your physical and emotional bodies. When incorporated in healing baths, this crystal has a tranquilizing effect.

Azurite

This crystal is effective for skin diseases; thus, it is recommended for individuals who possess a Type A personality. The use of the Azurite protects them against diseases of the internal organs caused by anxiety. You may also use this if your goal is to develop discipline.

Beryl

Use this crystal to combat laziness. It is also effective in curing a number of physical diseases such as optical disorders, inflamed glands and bowel cancer.

Bloodstone

Also known as Heliotrope, this crystal has a powerful grounding effect. Use it to help yourself get through heavily emotional situations. This crystal is also believed to be a powerful multipurpose cleanser and cure. Not only will it improve your circulation, it will also purify your bloodstream.

Calcite

This is also known as the "Transformation Stone". A Calcite of any hue may be used to cleanse your chakras. Invest in this crystal if you need help in recovering from a devastating emotional trauma. The Blue Calcite helps in stabilizing a quickening heartbeat. Likewise, it amplifies one's energy. Perhaps its most precious feature is that it facilitates communication between a person's physical, mental and spiritual self.

Carnelian

The Carnelian is a cure for apathy. It connects your lower chakras to your heart chakra. You may also use this to shield yourself against envy. If you need a boost in creativity, this crystal may prove to be valuable. It helps an individual connect with their sensual side. More importantly, the

Carnelian has the power to help you recover past-life experiences. It has an advancing effect toward the laws of karma.

Chalcedony

This is highly recommended for sensitive individuals with melancholic tendencies. It helps in lowering fever and aids in the treatment of a number of illnesses, from eye problems to gallstones to leukemia.

Chrysocolla

This crystal aids in balancing one's emotions. Use it when you are suffering from feelings of guilt and other nervous emotions. For pregnant women, the Chrysocolla ensures that labor and birth become easier. Likewise, it may be used by women suffering from diseases of the female reproductive system. Furthermore, for both men and women, this crystal facilitates clairvoyance.

Chrysolite

This is effective in fighting off viral infections and toxemia. It also brings about inspiration.

Chrysoprase

This crystal promotes reproductive health. Additionally, it's good for people suffering from gout. The Chrysoprase makes the user less inclined to hysteria and greed.

Citrine

This is also called the "Stone of Success". Invest in it if your goal is to achieve wealth and abundance. This crystal aids in increasing one's self-esteem. It is believed to be a lucky stone for business projects. Benefits for your physical body include improved health for the kidneys, the liver, the heart, the digestive system, the red and white corpuscles, and the muscles. This crystal is also often used in clearing the vibrations in the atmosphere. It also enhances the user's creativity. For individuals suffering from self-destructive behavior, the Citrine can protect them from themselves.

Diamond

Diamonds are effective against diseases of the brain as well as illnesses that affect the pituitary and the pineal glands. Use it when drawing out poisonous substances.

Diopsite and Enstatiate

This is used for cases of organ rejection specifically in transplant surgery. It also stimulates your heart, your kidneys and your lungs.

Emerald

This is also referred to as the "Stone of Loyalty". It opens up a person's heart chakra, making them more receptive to love. The Emerald has long been used against psychological illnesses and neurological disorders. This crystal is valuable in developing one's psychic and clairvoyant skills. It enables a person to have a deeper insight into their dreams. It also helps you keep in line with your life's purpose.

Fluorite

This is mainly used due to its calming effects on a person's emotions. However, it also has a strengthening effect on one's memory and concentration. This crystal may turn out to be a smart investment if your goal is to develop wisdom. It helps in alleviating and preventing pain. It is also effective in treating diseases of the skeletal system.

Fuchsite

This crystal increases your ability to reflect and to heal yourself. Additionally, it enables you to become physically and emotionally flexible.

Garnet

This is also popularly known as the "Stone of Health", curing anything from hemorrhage to hormonal imbalances. Use the Garnet to stimulate your Kundalini and to fuel your internal flame and creative power. This crystal may be used to ward off nightmares. It is also a known cure for depression.

Hematite

Its other name is the "Anti-stress Stone". It cleanses and purifies the blood. When a malicious individual sends negative energy your way, the Hematite causes this bad energy to bounce back towards its sender. This crystal also aids in Astral Projection. When attached to your back, it helps boost electromagnetic circulation.

Hemimorphite

This crystal protects a weak self-esteem. If you're the type of person who tends to carry negative feelings towards others, the Hemimorphite will aid in purifying your intentions.

Herkimer Diamond

You may use this crystal to enhance your dream state. It is popularly utilized in eliminating toxicity from the physical body. Moreover, the Herkimer Diamond makes a person more giving.

Jade

This crystal sparks ambition and aids in the accomplishment of your goals. It is also effective against diseases affecting vital organs such as the heart, the liver, and the kidneys. It aids in the treatment of illnesses associated with the spleen, the thyroid, and the parathyroid.

Jasper

The Yellow Jasper strengthens the tissues of the endocrine system. It also ensures proper etheric body alignment. Meanwhile, the Red Jasper may be used to fight infections of the stomach and the liver.

Kunzite

Use this crystal if you're struggling with alcohol addiction. This imbues a sense of well-being and mental peace upon the carrier; thus, it is utilized to prevent or treat schizophrenia and manic-depressive disorders. It is also used by individuals who suffer from epilepsy and by those who wish to prevent thyroid malignancy.

Labradorite

One of the most valuable uses of this crystal is for protecting, clarifying and balancing your aura. It keeps your aura free from energy leaks.

Lapis Lazuli

This crystal provides its carrier with mental clarity. Use it when you are having issues with self-acceptance.

Malachite

Use this crystal to achieve equilibrium in your right and left brain functions. Use it also to improve your eyesight and coordination. When used hand in hand with the rose quartz, this crystal helps in soothing and patching up a broken heart. The Malachite is an evil eye protector. It also removes radiation.

Moonstone

This crystal is highly recommended for individuals who are in need of emotional nurturing. Aside from encouraging inner growth, it will help you in nourishing your psychic abilities.

Morganite

This promotes the function of your parasympathetic nervous system, your larynx, and your thyroid.

Muscovite

This crystal is helpful in relieving energy blockages and in maintaining the perfect alignment of the chakras.

Obsidian

Use the Obsidian if you possess a gentle nature. This will keep you from being abused by others. In addition, this crystal has an anti-inflammatory effect.

Onyx

Invest in the Onyx if you need help in controlling your passion. The Onyx will help you maintain objective thinking while getting rid of pessimistic thoughts. It boosts cardiac health and strengthens your integumentary system. It also has stress-relieving properties.

Opal

The Cherry Opal is used for curing blood disorders. It is also believed to get rid of lethargy. Meanwhile, the dark opal is utilized for bone marrow health as well as for its grounding effects. The jelly opal increases your ability to absorb nutrients. It also stabilizes a person's mercurial moods. The light opal is known to prevent abdominal problems and for its ability to stimulate the white corpuscles.

Pearl

Aside from its beauty, the pearl is used against disorders of the GI tract. More importantly, though, it enables a person to be in command of their heart chakra.

Peridot

This crystal works by aligning your subtle bodies. It also provides the user with physical power. You may also utilize it to soothe wounded emotions.

Pyrite

This cleanses your upper respiratory tract. You can use this crystal when you're having respiratory problems.

Quartz

The clear quartz is popular for its ability to convert negative energy into positive energy. It repels harmful radiation so it is often worn as jewelry. If you're an artist suffering from creative blocks, the clear quartz can help awaken your creative side. All you need to do is to gaze upon the crystal for a few minutes. Also known as the "love stone", the rose quartz opens up your heart chakra. Placing the crystal on your heart chakra for about fifteen minutes yields a comforting effect. It heals emotional wounds and promotes self-acceptance. The smoky quartz is recommended for individuals who are experiencing burnout or extreme stress.

Ruby

This is another crystal that is known as a heart chakra opener. It also helps you maintain balance between your emotional and spiritual goals. Additionally, pregnant women may use a ruby to prevent having miscarriages.

Rutile

This crystal relieves psychological blockages that are the result of traumatic events in one's childhood.

Sapphire

This is used primarily for achieving inner peace and spiritual enlightenment. It has also been proven to be valuable in astral projection and clairvoyance.

Sardonyx

This is used as a protection against anxiety and grief.

Selenite

This crystal enables you to develop telepathy and attain a clear state of mind.

Smithsonite

The Smithsonite enables the unification of astral and emotional bodies. It also assists in balancing your viewpoint.

Sodalite

This crystal does not only awaken your third eye, but also conditions your mind so that it will be ready to receive "the inner sight". In addition, it helps moderate mental noise.

Spinel

This helps detoxify the body. Apart from that, it can also treat problems affecting the lower extremities.

Sugalite

This crystal opens up your crown chakra. It makes you more receptive to visions. Apart from increasing altruism, it also shields you from negative vibrations.

Tiger's Eye

Use this if you have an issue with responsibility. This crystal also helps your mind to focus.

Topaz

This is recommended for people who are suffering from poor appetite. This crystal boosts tissue regeneration. Moreover, the topaz helps to rejuvenate your spirit. Other benefits of this crystal include the treatment of certain diseases from STDs to tuberculosis.

Tourmaline

The black tourmaline is suggested for individuals suffering from dyslexia. This crystal is also effective in neutralizing distorted energies. The pink tourmaline protects you from victimization. For women, this crystal helps to enhance their beauty. The rubellite tourmaline is a gemstone used to aid in fertility. Meanwhile, the watermelon tourmaline heals the heart chakra. It also provides the person with a sense of security. Use it if you wish to improve your sense of humor as well.

Turquoise

This is also referred to as the "protection stone". It stops you from being distracted by others; thus, allowing you to be free to focus on your own accomplishments. Wear it around your throat chakra to enhance your communication skills. Use it when you're having difficulty in voicing out the truth. This gemstone is also favored by a lot of people because it is believed to slow the aging process.

Unakite

The Green Unakite helps you to become more grounded. It also provides you with the strength to recover from disappointments. Meanwhile, the Pink Unakite aids in smoother movement.

Chapter 8:
Crystals vs. Gemstones

Definition, Composition and Uses

Contrary to what most people think, crystals and gemstones are not the same. A gemstone is defined as a beautiful stone with zero to minimal flaws. They are cut and polished and are usually utilized to create jewelry and other decorative ornaments. They are also treated as collectibles. Gemstones are rare minerals derived from the earth and some may be categorized as crystals. A diamond is an example of a gemstone with a crystalline structure. Such structure is responsible for providing the diamond with its extraordinary beauty. It is necessary to note that while some gemstones may be crystals, not all crystals are gemstones.

Some gemstones such as diamonds and rubies consist of mineral bases. On the other hand, there are gemstones that are made up of organic bases. An example of which is the amber (fossilized tree resin) and jet (coal). Note that generally, minerals are a great deal harder compared to other substances that may comprise a precious stone.

Crystals are defined as pure materials with atoms, molecules and ions that are naturally fashioned in a regular and repeating geometric pattern extending in three spatial dimensions. This pattern can easily be seen in larger crystals such as garnet and quartz. Meanwhile, the structures of some crystals such as the agate and the chalcedony may only be observed with the aid of a microscope.

In order to achieve its symmetrical shape, a crystal's unit cells should stack flawlessly and should be devoid of gaps. Crystallization refers to the process through which crystals are formed. This is otherwise known as solidification. That said, not all crystals come in solid form. Crystals have various uses from making jewelry, to healing, to scientific research. They are also often used as materials for vases and dishes.

Classification and Pricing

Gemstones are typically more expensive than crystals and are either precious or semi-precious. Examples of precious gemstones are sapphires and emeralds. Crystals, on the other hand, are not always precious. Examples are snowflakes and salt. A gemstone's price depends highly upon its rarity, its cut, its color, its hardness and its composition.

When classifying gemstones, the chemical composition and the crystal's structure need to be considered. Meanwhile, crystals are grouped according to shape. They may be cubic, tertragonal, monoclinic, orthombic, or rhombohedral.

Characteristics

When dealing with gemstones, you need to pay attention to the following characteristics: refractive index, hardness, and specific gravity. You also need to determine the luster, the dispersion, the cleavage and the fracture. When dealing with crystals, you have to look at the shape and the atom composition of the crystal. You also need to check the bonds and defects.

Color

Gemstones come in various colors from red to green, etc. Compared to them, crystals are lighter and often translucent. The latter's color is influenced by the transmission of light through the crystal.

Cleaning

You should refrain from using cleansers that contain alcohol in cleaning a non-crystal gemstone. Doing so will damage the stone. Overall, it is recommended to invest in gemstones that possess a crystalline structure.

Chapter 9:
How to Cleanse Crystals?

When using crystals for healing, you need to cleanse your crystals regularly to ensure that they remain at the highest vibration. This is necessary to maintain their power to absorb and provide energy. After purchasing a crystal, you need to cleanse it immediately prior to using it. Having been exposed to multiple environments, events, and people, the crystal has encountered several types of energies. It's possible that the new crystal may have harbored some negative energy which you'll need to get rid of first.

Cleansing through Sound and Singing Bowls

Cleanse small crystals by placing them inside crystal singing bowls. If your crystals are too big to fit inside the bowl, just place them beside it. Playing with the bowl will emit beautiful music, which will vibrate throughout the room. This vibration is responsible for driving out the negative energies from your crystals while also lifting their vibrations. At the same time, the sound will fill your room with positive vibrations. Perform this for a few minutes.

Cleansing with the Use of White Light

Prior to cleansing natural crystals, close your eyes and utter a petition to your god/goddess or spirit or ask the universe to provide you with white light. In your mind's eye, visualize your physical form filling up with white light. Feel this extra energy as it begins to grow inside you.

Then, open your eyes and consciously send the white light towards the crystals. You may perform a sweeping motion with your hands to direct the light. Ask your god/goddess, spirit, or the universe to transform the negative energies in the crystals into positive energy with the aid of the white light. Aside from crystal cleansing, you may also use this method to boost your own vibration or that of the surroundings'.

Cleansing Crystals through Smudging

To cleanse your crystals through this method, you'll need some loose white sage leaves. Alternatively, you may purchase smudge sticks from stores. Some sage smudge sticks also contain lavender or other aromatic herbs. These added herbs may possess healing properties that you may also benefit from.

You may choose to hold your crystals over the sage smoke or hold the smudge stick close to where your crystals are kept. Make sure that the air surrounding the crystals is filled with the sage essence. Not only will the smoke cleanse the crystals, it will also purify the room. Professional healers perform this method after using their crystal wands on a client.

Cleansing Crystals with Running Water

One of the easiest methods for cleansing crystals is by holding them under running water. Trust your intuition in determining whether the negative energies have been completely washed away.

Cleansing Crystals with Saltwater

Soak the crystals in saltwater for several hours. You may also leave them overnight. Then, rinse them with the use of cool running water. Note that not all crystals may safely be cleansed with saltwater. Refrain from using the saltwater cleansing method on crystals that are porous or on those that possess high metal or high water content. Examples of crystals that should not come in contact with saltwater or salt are hematite and Lapis Lazuli.

Cleansing Crystals with Salt

This is otherwise known as the dry method. Do this by burying the crystals beneath the sea salt. Leave them there for a few hours. Afterwards, you'll need to dispose of the salt. This is because all the negative energies from the crystals have been absorbed by it so you wouldn't want the salt to be anywhere near you.

You may also perform the non-direct dry method in cleansing crystals like Hematite and Lapis Lazuli. Place some salt in a glass bowl but fill it only halfway. Afterwards, procure another empty glass and place it inside the bowl, submerging it in salt. Then, place your crystals inside the glass. You may or may not add water into the glass.

Cleansing Crystals through Burial

Another way of cleaning your crystals is by burying them in the earth. That said, crystals that are damaged by water cannot be cleansed through this method. Rainwater may seep through to where your crystals are buried and then damage the stones. After burying your crystals, place a mark on the site.

Cleansing Crystals with Rice

For this method you may choose either white or brown rice. All you need to do is to fill a flat bowl with rice and place your crystals on top. Leave them there overnight. Similar to the dry method of cleansing with salt, the rice will absorb the crystals' negative energy so refrain from reusing the rice.

Chapter 10:
How to Clear your Chakras to Make Crystal Healing More Effective

You can use crystals to activate, heal, energize, and balance your chakras or your energy centers. However, to make them more receptive to the energy emitted by crystals, you first need to take certain steps to clear your chakras.

Chakra Meditation

The goal of chakra meditation is to slow down your physical vibration. Your chakras may be activated but they may also be wide open. This makes them susceptible to various external vibrational patterns. Such energies tend to pull in slow frequency forces which, in turn, linger in your personal sphere and reduce your energy.

When this happens, your chakras and the body organs associated with them will suffer from too much pressure.

- Begin the chakra meditation by allowing yourself to relax in a sitting position. Your weight should be balanced in the center. Your spine should be erect so that your chakras are properly aligned, allowing the energy to flow properly.

- Focus on your breathing. Feel the air moving in and out of your system.

- Visualize a white fluid light (to symbolize the energy). Imagine it flowing from your crown chakra all the way down toward your lower chakras. Feel the sensation of the warm light touching and passing through each of your chakras.

- After meditating, perform a grounding exercise. You may do this by imagining that you are a tree with roots spreading and clinging to the earth. Feel the energy coming from the earth being absorbed by your roots, filling and fortifying your entire being.

Yoga

You may also clear your chakras though kundalini and other types of yoga. The moving and the stretching of your body also move and stretch the energy within. When this happens, accumulated negative energy is drawn away from its area of concentration.

Detoxify your Environment

A messy room or workspace can mess up your chakras as well. Organize your home and your office. Get rid of unnecessary stuff especially those with bad memories or negative feelings attached to them. Organizing your space will enable the energy to flow freely and effectively in the room. As much as possible, stick to natural materials and minimize the use of synthetic furniture. Electrical appliances interfere with your personal energy field. While you can't totally get rid of your gadgets, you can do little things like minimizing their presence in the bedroom or by refraining from sleeping with your mobile phone.

Acupuncture and Massage

These practices are also done to mobilize stagnant energy.

Heat

Heat has a relaxing effect on your muscles, enabling the negative energy to trickle out of your body. You may do this by indulging in a sauna or whirlpool.

Forgiveness and Acceptance

Energy blockages are a result of repressed emotions that have been accumulated. Think of all the people who have done you wrong and silently thank them. They have provided you with valuable lessons in life. It's not just other people that you need to forgive. You need to learn to forgive yourself as well. Accept your flaws and limitations. Look within yourself for positive traits and ways through which you can enhance them.

Chapter 11:
Different Ways that Crystals can be Used for Healing

Wear your crystals.

You can harness the healing powers of crystals simply by wearing them as jewelry. Alternatively, you may carry the crystals in a tiny pouch to be pinned inside your clothing. Aside from healing you, these crystals will also serve as protective amulets. To increase its effectiveness, wear the crystal on or near the body part that requires healing. For instance, if you're suffering from a thyroid disease or from an underactive throat chakra, wear a choker with a turquoise pendant around your neck. Some healers believe that carrying crystals on the left side of your body offers greater aid in receiving energy.

Place them under your pillow.

Keeping crystals beneath your pillow will enable you to sleep well and get rid of bad dreams. You'll notice that you will feel more energized upon waking. If you want to be able to recall your dreams, place a garnet under your pillow. Individuals who are interested in astral travel can also keep crystals under their pillows.

Incorporate them in your bath.

Add crystals like the rose quartz and clear quartz to your bathwater or arrange them around the bath tub to benefit from their soothing effects. Doing so will also aid you in cleansing not just your body but also your non-physical form. Furthermore, the crystals will absorb the negative energies that you have absorbed and accumulated throughout the day.

Use them during meditation.

The structure of the crystal itself possesses the power to add balance and stillness into your life. During meditation, hold the healing crystals inside your palms. Alternatively, you may simply place the crystals in front of you.

Make crystal elixirs or gem water.

Make gem water by submerging gemstones in a bowl of natural spring water. Leave it there to soak overnight. Note that there are crystals that are highly toxic and should not be ingested or absorbed by the skin. Gem water may be added full strength to your bath water or you may use it as a spraying mist for the body or for the house.

If you really want to make a crystal elixir, submerge the crystals in a bowl of natural spring water. Then, expose the bowl to direct sunlight for two hours. After that, transfer the concentrated essence (which is known as the crystal's mother essence) to a bottle so that it's filled halfway. Next, fill the rest of the bottle with brandy.

Obtain another empty bottle. Place a few drops of the crystal's mother essence in it. Then fill the bottle halfway with clean drinking water. Afterwards, fill the rest of the bottle with brandy.

Only by following this formula will the crystal essence be safe to drink. That is, unless you're using a highly toxic crystal (to be discussed in the next chapter), then you shouldn't even think of making an elixir at all. Consume crystal elixirs in very small doses. Alternatively, you may inhale the essence.

Place them directly on your chakras.

Each chakra has a distinct color. As a general rule, crystals that are of the same base color as a chakra will work best with that energy center. For example, since the seventh chakra's (crown chakra) color is violet, it responds well to amethysts. Meanwhile, the pink heart chakra may be activated by a pink-colored crystal like rose quartz.

Chapter 12:
Toxic Crystals to Avoid

When making elixirs or massage oils from healing crystals, you need to ensure that the stones you are using do not possess toxic substances that may seep into the water. These substances are usually micro-minerals that our bodies require to survive. However, when introduced to the body in larger amounts, they yield toxic effects. Take copper, for instance. Crystals with copper content include Cuprite, Bronchanite, Gem Silica, Cavansite, and Atacamite. Magnetite carries large quantities of iron.

There are crystals that are so toxic that you should avoid handling them with bare hands. Examples of these are crystals that contain arsenic such as Realgar. Wear protective gloves before handling crystals that contain mercury such as Cinnabar. To be safe, always wash your hands thoroughly with soap and water after working with minerals. Be careful when using Zircon which contains zirconium and is radioactive. Another radioactive crystal is Torbenite. Beware of keeping artificially irradiated crystals. To be safe, stay away from smoky quartz with an artificially dark color, tourmaline which possesses a very deep pink hue, Kunzite with deep pigments, colored diamonds, and deeply colored Topaz.

Some crystals are not poisonous per se, but may be toxic when used in a certain way. For instance, ingesting elixirs from stones that contain lead such as Vanadanite and Galena is extremely dangerous to one's health. Refrain also from making elixirs out of crystals that contain aluminum such as Variscite, Vesuvianite, Iolite, Wavellite, Tanzanite, Sunstone, Dumortierite, Prehnite, Stilbite, and Staurolite. Moldavite contains aluminum oxide as well. Psiomelane has barium. Meanwhile, Garnierite contains nickel.

Some crystals carry more than one toxic substance. Auricalcite, for example, contains both zinc and copper that are not toxic to the body in certain doses but should not be ingested in large amounts. Adamite and Mohawkite are highly toxic because they contain both copper and arsenic. The same goes with Ajoite which has both aluminum and copper. Wulfenite includes both lead and molybdenum. Atibnite has lead and antimony. Angelite carries lead and sulfur. Covellite comprises of copper and sulfur. Other sulfur-containing crystals are Boji stones and Markasite.

Note that some crystals may be toxic when in the raw form but are safe in the high polished form. Tiger's Eye, in its fibrous form, contains asbestos. The same can be said of Serpentine. Other asbestos-containing crystals include Actinolite and Tremolite. The Selenite may not be toxic but it is friable; therefore, when used in elixirs, small shards of the crystal may break off in the water. Some crystals like the Hematite are not toxic but will rust.

It's possible to find trapped-in toxic dust and fumes in Amber crystals. There are crystals than contain cyanobacteria and cyanotoxins such as the Stromalite. Corals may contain water pollutants and bacteria. The same goes with the Mother of Pearl. Before working with minerals, especially if you're planning to ingest them, consult a mineralogist or a geological professional. When you're in doubt about the safety of a certain stone, perform the indirect method of making crystal elixirs. Also, refrain from drinking, eating or smoking while working with potentially toxic crystals.

Chapter 13:
Crystals and their Use in Religions

Most people may not know this but crystals have played a great role in all religions. The Bible, the Quran, and several other religious scriptures have mentioned crystals more than once. In the Hebrew Bible, the Priestly Breastplate worn by the Israelites' High Priest consists of twelve different minerals which represent the 12 tribes. In the Quran, the Fourth Heaven is said to consist of garnet. In Hinduism, the Kalpa Tree, which symbolizes an offering to the gods, is believed to be composed of precious stones.

In Buddhism, a 7th century writing revealed that near the Neem Tree where Siddhartha performed his meditation, was a Throne of Diamond where the Kalpa Buddha rested. In Jainism, the Divine Commander Harinegamesi took and cleansed fourteen precious stones and used them to assist him in his transformations.

The use of crystals can be traced back to the time of the ancient Sumerians. They utilized crystals in order to create magic formulas. In ancient Egypt, priests made use of crystals such as emerald, clear quartz, turquoise, and Lapis Lazuli as amulets for health and protection. The topaz and the peridot were used to expel evil spirits. In ancient Mexico, green crystals like emerald were used in burials (sometimes as jade masks) because they were believed to represent the heart of the dead.

In ancient Greece, amethysts were used by men as amulets to protect themselves from the effects of drunkenness. The Hematite, which possesses a color like that of blood, was linked to the God of War. Soldiers used to rub this crystal over their bodies before engaging in battle because they believed that it would make them invincible in the battlefield. Likewise, Greek sailors donned amulets which were believed to aid in a safe voyage.

In ancient China, emperors were buried wearing an armor fashioned from jade. Up until today, from regions in China to certain places in South America, the latter is regarded as a powerful healing stone. From 250 years ago, the Māori people of New Zealand passed Jade pendants from one generation to the next because they were believed to signify the spirits of their ancestors.

Though the Christian church forbade the people from using crystal amulets in 355 AD, gemstones maintained their popularity. In the 12th century, for instance, sapphire was often used in fashioning ecclesiastical rings. Before that, in the 11th century, the Bishop of Rennes attested to the power of the Agate. According to him, anyone who uses this crystal becomes more favorable in the eyes of God. The Red Garnet was also often used to symbolize the sacrifice of Christ.

The dawn of the New Age in the 80's brought back a great deal of attention to the use of crystals in obtaining the assistance of gods/goddesses, spirits, and angels. While certain people may claim that crystals are evil and are tools that the devil/evil spirits use to communicate with us, it is important to remember that crystals/minerals are living beings and as part of the universe, they are considered as intrinsically good.

Chapter 14:
Crystals for Psychic Healing

As mentioned earlier, there are certain crystals that can help awaken your psychic abilities or open your third eye, but apart from that, crystals can also provide you with the ability of psychic healing.

Heal Yourself and Others

Whether it's a physical, mental, emotional or spiritual illness that you or your loved one is suffering from, you may use crystals to help things get better. You need not have direct contact with the patient. One way to perform psychic healing with crystals is by creating a crystal grid.

Choose a location in your home where the crystal grid will remain safe and untouched. Next, purify the room by burning loose-leaf white sage.

Then, select the crystals that you want to use. Allow your intuition to guide you in choosing. Now that you know the different crystals and their purposes, you should have an idea as to which stones will work best with your intention.

Arrange the stones with this intention in mind. Think of yourself or of the person who you want to heal. It would be best if you can write down the intention on a piece of paper to be placed in the heart of the grid.

Be sure to arrange the crystals from the outside moving in. Refrain from disturbing the grid for at least forty days.

Too much work? You may also heal your loved ones or yourself by simply visualizing/forming a healing cloak around the person/yourself. In your mind's eye, wrap the person/yourself with a bright light that is of the same color of the healing crystal. For example, if the person is suffering from abdominal problems, heal their solar plexus chakra by envisioning the yellow color of the Citrine crystal. You may also follow the same procedure in forming a cloak of protection around yourself or another person.

Neutralize Psychic Attacks

A psychic attack refers to negative energy that someone, either consciously or unconsciously, sends your way. The common reason for intentional psychic attacks is jealousy. However, it's also possible for a person to unintentionally project negative thoughts if they are currently "in a dark place". Symptoms that you are suffering from a psychic attack include nightmares, exhaustion, physical pain, lethargy, depression, and a horrible sensation of being watched. The worst symptom is a feeling that mimics the sensation of having a heart attack.

Another is when the victim feels the urge to commit suicide. Awful as this may sound, it should provide you with some sense of relief to know that crystals such as Ametrine can help in neutralizing psychic attacks. You may also use Ametrine to protect yourself during astral travel. A black tourmaline crystal in quartz will counteract psychic attacks while enhancing your well-being. It is also used to hasten one's recovery from a previous psychic attack.

To prevent psychic attacks from occurring in the first place, protect yourself with amethysts. The high level spiritual vibration of this crystal transmutes negative energy to love. The ruby may be used to prevent both psychic attacks and psychic vampirism. Psychic vampirism occurs in parasitic relationships where the malicious party feeds off of your life force. Aventurine shields your heart chakra from psychic vampires who want to feed off of your heart energy.

Conclusion

Thank you again for downloading this book!

I hope this book was able to help you learn more about crystal healing!

The next step is to put this information to use, and begin using crystal healing in your own life!

Finally, if you enjoyed this book, please take the time to share your thoughts and post a review on Amazon. It'd be greatly appreciated!

Thank you and good luck!

www.ingramcontent.com/pod-product-compliance
Lightning Source LLC
LaVergne TN
LVHW021737060526
838200LV00052B/3329